HOW DO WE KNOW ABOUT MARCO POLO?

Marco Polo lived from 1254 to 1324, and his famous journey to
China and other Asian countries lasted from 1271 to 1295. In 1298,
Marco was captured during a naval battle between his home city of
Venice and the nearby city of Genoa, and he became a prisoner of
war. While in prison, he dictated the story of his travels to another
prisoner, Rustichello da Pisa. Rustichello was a writer of romances
– adventure stories about knights and ladies. Did he 'improve'
Marco's story to make it more exciting? Well, he may have done,
but most experts think the story that Rustichello wrote down is
pretty accurate.

   Rustichello probably wrote the story in French at first – because
romances were usually written in French – but it was soon
translated into many other languages. The oldest copies of the book
are manuscripts (handwritten copies), because printing was not yet
known in Europe. Printing had already been invented in China –
but, strangely enough, Marco doesn't mention it in his book!

Author:
Jacqueline Morley studied English at
Oxford University. She has taught English and
History, and now works as a freelance writer.
She has written historical fiction and non-fiction
for children.

Artist:
David Antram was born in Brighton, England,
in 1958. He studied at Eastbourne College of Art
and then worked in advertising for fifteen years
before becoming a full-time artist. He has
illustrated many children's non-fiction books.

Series creator:
David Salariya was born in Dundee, Scotland.
He has illustrated a wide range of books and has
created and designed many new series for
publishers in the UK and overseas. David
established The Salariya Book Company in 1989.
He lives in Brighton with his wife, illustrator
Shirley Willis, and their son Jonathan.

Editor: **Stephen Haynes**

Editorial Assistant: **Mark Williams**

PAPER FROM
SUSTAINABLE
FORESTS

Published in Great Britain in MMIX by
Book House, an imprint of
The Salariya Book Company Ltd
25 Marlborough Place, Brighton BN1 1UB
www.salariya.com
www.book-house.co.uk

HB ISBN-13: 978-1-906714-13-0
PB ISBN-13: 978-1-906714-14-7

S A L A R I Y A

1 3 5 7 9 8 6 4 2

A CIP catalogue record for this book is available
from the British Library.

Printed and bound in China.

Visit our website at **www.book-house.com**
or go to **www.salariya.com** for **free** electronic versions of:
You Wouldn't Want to be an Egyptian Mummy!
You Wouldn't Want to be a Roman Gladiator!
Avoid Joining Shackleton's Polar Expedition!
Avoid Sailing on a 19th-Century Whaling Ship!

Avoid exploring with Marco Polo!

Written by
Jacqueline Morley

Illustrated by
David Antram

Created and designed by
David Salariya

The Danger Zone

BOOK HOUSE

Contents

Introduction

It's 1269. You are a servant to the Polos, a wealthy merchant family in the great Italian trading port of Venice. You've grown up as companion to young master Marco, who's 15 now – just a bit younger than you. Marco's mother is dead and his father, Niccolò, has not been seen for years. He sailed away on a trading trip with his brother Maffeo. That was in 1260. After all this time, most people assume they're both dead. Imagine the thrill, then, when they suddenly reappear – and with such a story to tell! It's the beginning of a great adventure for you and Marco that takes you to places you had no idea existed. But if you'd known how dangerous it would be, and that you'd be away for more than 20 years, would you really have wanted to explore with Marco Polo?

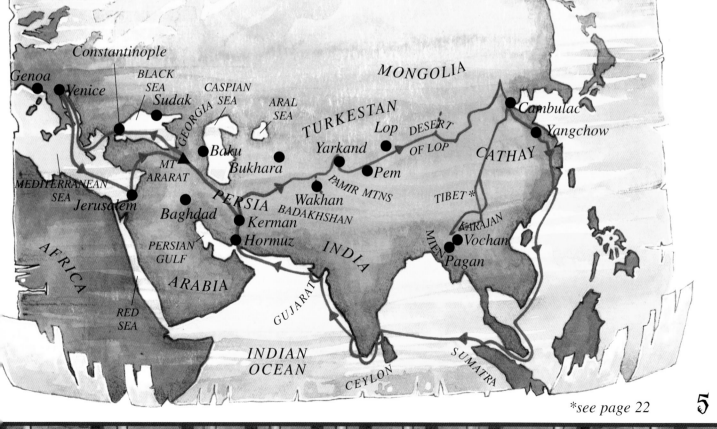

*see page 22

An unexpected return

Niccolò

Maffeo

Marco

O ver supper you hear the brothers' story. They went first to the great trading centre of Constantinople,* where Arab dealers bring goods from eastern lands. Like everyone else in Europe, the brothers knew next to nothing of these lands, but they decided to try trading in Mongol territory, to the north-east. Local wars then forced them to travel into central Asia. From there they went on to Cathay,** a vast land in the distant east. They met its mighty ruler, Kublai Khan, supreme lord of all the Mongols. He has given the Polos a message for their supreme lord, the Pope, and sent them home to deliver it.

*present-day Istanbul, in Turkey
**China

The brothers' story

FROM CONSTANTINOPLE, the Polos sailed their galley across the Black Sea to Sudak in the Crimea. Here, like other Venetians, they had a trading depot.

THE LAND BEYOND SUDAK is ruled by the Mongols, a warlike people who rule most of Asia. War between rival Mongol rulers blocked the Polos' way home.

6

THE POLOS had to make a huge detour east. After much hard travel they reached the city of Bukhara. Here they met an envoy to the court of Kublai Khan, who offered to take them to the Khan.

IT TOOK A YEAR, but at last they knelt before the Mongol ruler. He was most curious about the lands they came from, and asked many questions about their Christian religion.

RETURNING through blizzards and swollen rivers has taken them three years. Now they learn that the Pope has died. They cannot deliver the Khan's message until a new Pope has been elected.

Setting off

The Khan has asked the Pope for holy oil from Jerusalem, and a hundred learned men to teach him all about the West. A new Pope is chosen in 1271 and the Polos can at last set off, with costly papal gifts and greetings, for Cathay. You can't believe your luck when they decide to take Marco with them, and he wants you to go as well!

After collecting the holy oil from Jerusalem, you head north and east to avoid Egyptian invaders. Then you start the dusty journey southwards through Persia.* The ways are unsafe. Each village you pass through supplies an escort to the next village – but can you trust the escort?

now Iran

Quiver!

Chatter!

I've just remembered something I have to do at home.

THE POPE hasn't been able to muster a hundred learned men. He's only sent two friars. They don't get far. The trip has barely started when you learn that invaders from Egypt are ravaging the area just ahead. The cowardly friars flee back home at once.

YOU PASS MOUNT ARARAT in Lesser Armenia.* According to tradition, this is where Noah's ark landed – but you can't see it.

now in Turkey

Splosh!

Handy hint

That oil that comes out of the ground is good for treating mange in camels.

It's true! I feel much better now.

AT BAKU near the Georgian border, oil gushes from the ground! You can't use it for cooking, but it burns well in lamps.

20 per cent off – that's my last offer.

This way, masters!

AFTER CROSSING miles of desert prickly with thorn bushes, you reach Kerman, famous for the turquoises mined nearby. The Polos do some successful haggling for them.

Bringers of darkness

You've now joined a caravan of merchants, as it's safer to stick with other people. South of Kerman you enter a danger zone where people live at the mercy of bandits called the Karaunas. Some people believe the Karaunas can use devilish arts and can create darkness whenever they wish. Sure enough, the sky grows suddenly dark* and the bandits rush upon you. Apart from the Polos and yourself, only three travellers escape. The rest are either killed or sold as slaves.

Fat-tailed sheep

YOU ESCAPE the Karaunas by fleeing to a nearby town.

All the towns and villages of the region have massive walls to keep marauders out. Even so, the local people never feel safe. Once outside the town walls, their animals may be seized, their old folk killed and the young dragged off into slavery.

I don't think they like the look of us.

Let us in! Please!

The darkness may have been caused by 'dry fog' – very fine bits of sand suspended in the air.

THE BEASTS people keep here are quite different from those at home. There are sheep as tall as donkeys, that store vast amounts of fat in their tails, and beautiful white oxen with humps on their shoulders, that kneel down to be loaded.

White ox

Shaky ships

A SCORCHING WIND from the plains blows over Hormuz in summer. It gets so unbearably hot that people only survive by staying neck-deep in water.

You've now reached Hormuz, a busy port on the Persian Gulf where all sorts of precious wares from India and Africa arrive. The Polo brothers plan to board a ship there and reach Cathay by sea. They think this will be quicker than the land route. As you near the coast, the heat gets worse and worse. By March, all around Hormuz every leaf is shrivelled.

THEY SAY that an army caught by this wind was shrivelled to death. The corpses were so dry that when people tried to shift them the arms snapped off.

MARCO falls seriously ill. You are all worried about him, but the brothers are also anxious about their goods. The ruler of Hormuz seizes the property of foreigners who die there.

YOU'LL BE GLAD to leave Hormuz. The city is filled with a constant wailing noise. Whenever there is a death, the women of the family mourn loudly every day for four years. The noise never stops.

At the docks the Polos get a shock. To a Venetian, the local ships don't look at all safe. Their planks aren't nailed down, but stitched together with coconut fibre. And there's no deck – just skins thrown over the cargo. The Polos would rather go by land than sail in one of these, and that means turning back.

Handy hint

Avoid the local bread. The brackish water gives it a nasty taste.

The finest ship afloat! I only wish I could go with you...

13

On the roof of the world

You have to go back to Kerman to join the land route, which leads you over the barren plains of central Persia and into Turkestan, where chains of mountains stretch in all directions. Marco soon recovers in the fresh mountain air.

From there on, you're climbing all the time. You never could have imagined paths so steep. You finally reach a wide, grassy plateau, high in the Pamir Mountains. It must be the top of the world! It will take 12 days to cross, and you'll have to carry everything you need, for there's no-one up here to supply anything. It's bitterly cold, which must be why you can't get the fire to burn well. The flames are so feeble the stew won't cook.* The others are impatient for their meal, but the meat's going to be tough.

MUCH OF THE ROUTE is desert. There's no water fit to drink and, worse still, you have to ride a camel. They've got bad tempers and foul teeth, and riding one makes you feel seasick.

> Where d'you think you're going?

IN BADAKHSHAN (a region in Turkestan) rubies are mined, but only for the king. Anyone caught exporting them is executed.

FROM BADAKHSHAN, you follow the Oxus River up through many narrow passes into Wakhan, the gateway to the Pamirs.

DANGEROUS WOLVES lurk in the Pamirs. At night you see their eyes glittering in the light of the camp fire.

The stew wouldn't soften because at very high altitudes it takes longer for things to cook – but this wasn't understood in the 13th century.

PAMIR WILD SHEEP* have enormous horns. Their bones are everywhere because the wolves kill them.

*sometimes called Marco Polo sheep

Handy hint

Your beasts may drink from a brackish water supply if you add flour to it.

I've really worked up an appetite.

I'm doing my best here!

PFFFF!!!

15

The great desert of Lop

Now you really wish you'd stayed at home. In the town of Lop they warned you about this terrible desert.* They say it's full of evil spirits that fill the air with noises: music, drums, the clash of weapons and the thunder of galloping horses. Phantom voices call travellers by name, luring them away so they are never seen again.** You daren't look round, but you're sure the demons are behind you now. You can hear them distinctly. You'll never stand another month of this – but that's how long it's going to take to cross this desert.

IN THE PROVINCE OF YARKAND, beyond the Pamirs, many people seem to have one foot larger than the other. Many also suffer from a goitre (a neck swelling). Marco thinks this is caused by something in the water.***

*now called the Gobi Desert
**The noises are caused by the slipping of sand on the dunes; they can be quite loud and eerie.
***It is often caused by a lack of iodine in the body.

poor things!

Got one!

IN THE REGION OF PEM there are rivers in which you can find lumps of jade if you hunt long enough.

Howl!

Handy hint

Before you go to bed, point a sign in the direction you're travelling – the wind will erase your tracks during the night.

Pull yourself together, man. It's all in your imagination.

Neat!

Ting!

A GUIDE tells you to hang bells on your animals. Otherwise you'll never find them if they stray. Shifting desert sand will hide their tracks.

BEYOND THE DESERT you reach the first Chinese villages. Marco is fascinated by a huge statue of a Buddha.

17

Before the Khan

As soon as he hears that the Polos are in Cathay, Kublai Khan sends escorts to bring you to him. The Khan's presence is awe-inspiring and his expression is shrewd. He sits with a live tiger at his feet. He takes the Pope's gifts graciously, but is disappointed to receive no learned men. He had hoped to learn a great deal from them about the politics, religions and sciences of other lands. He understands that knowledge is power!

BEFORE they conquered China, the Mongols were herdsmen wandering the Asian steppes. Their portable homes were made of animal skins.

NOW the Mongols live in luxury. The Khan has many palaces and even a portable bamboo hunting lodge (above) that looks just like a palace.

Don't tread on the threshold of the Khan's Great Hall. It causes bad luck and you'll get a beating.

At Your Majesty's service!

At least she's quieter than the last one.

THE KHAN loves all kinds of hunting, especially falconry. He rides to the hunt in a pavilion carried by elephants.

IT IS SAID that the Khan's magicians can make the weather do whatever suits him, and that they can make his drinking cup float to him through the air.

IN ADDITION to four official wives, the Khan has countless carefully chosen concubines. The ladies of the court check each candidate to ensure that she has sweet breath and does not snore.

19

The wonderful city

The wonders of Cambulac,* the Khan's capital, are beyond belief, it is so vast and so bustling with people. It is all newly built, laid out on a grid plan. Wide avenues are lined with shops of every kind. Wherever you look you see fine inns and houses, and palaces with large gardens.

NO-ONE is going to believe this! The people here use paper instead of coins as money! It is issued by the Khan and printed with his seal. Everyone treats it as if it were as good as gold or silver.

*or Khan-balik; now called Beijing

Cambulac makes you feel ashamed of Venice's crooked alleys and smelly canals. And as for wealth – no-one at home could imagine the amount of trade that goes on here. Every day 1,000 cartloads of raw silk are brought to the city for weaving, and all the treasures of India and Cathay – precious stones, pearls, the finest cloths – flood into its markets.

Handy hint

Don't go out at night after the great bell has rung, or you'll be jailed as a suspicious person.

THE KHAN'S VAST PALACE complex contains many buildings, roofed with tiles as bright as crystal. The reception hall, covered inside with gold and silver and painted dragons, is so big that 6,000 men can feast in it.

We could do with some of this back home.

THE CITY WALLS are 39 km (24 miles) round, with 12 well-guarded gates. Each of the 12 districts inside the gates is bigger than the whole of Venice.

ANOTHER SURPRISE: black stones that burn like logs and stay lit all night. They are used a lot in the bath houses. People here take at least three baths a week!

THE POSTAL SERVICE is a wonder. Europe has nothing like it. Riders doing 40-km (25-mile) relays deliver urgent post. Runners carry ordinary mail.

21

Marco's missions

The Khan was impressed by the lively way Marco described your journey here. Observant people are useful to him. The Khan needs to keep firm control of all the lands he's conquered, and for that he needs good information. So he has kept the Polos in his service, and for some years now he has been sending Marco to distant regions to make detailed reports. He's on a trip now to Tibet, Karajan and Mien,* with you in tow.

Tibet is modern Szechwan (Sichuan), Karajan is Yunnan, and Mien is Burma (Myanmar). The country that is now called Tibet is an entirely different place, and Marco didn't go there.

IN TIBET there are forests of giant bamboo canes. You try cutting some for firewood. When lit, the green canes explode with such deafening bangs that your horses bolt! Next night you tether and blindfold the horses before you light the fire.

IN KARAJAN there are dreadful serpents ten paces long and as wide as a barrel, which could eat you in one gulp. They can only be killed by sinking sharp blades in the ground, which slit their bellies as they crawl along.

AT VOCHAN, in Zardandan, when a woman has a baby, her husband takes it to bed with him. He stays there for 40 days while his wife waits on him and does all her usual work.

KUIJU PROVINCE* is full of tigers that swim out and snatch fishermen from their boats.
Experts are not sure where this was.

The gold and silver temples of Pagan in Mien

Handy hint

Drinking the bile of those man-eating serpents is said to be a sure cure for the bite of a mad dog.

And I used to think Venice had all the best buildings!

A voyage to India

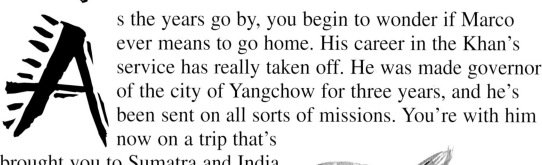

As the years go by, you begin to wonder if Marco ever means to go home. His career in the Khan's service has really taken off. He was made governor of the city of Yangchow for three years, and he's been sent on all sorts of missions. You're with him now on a trip that's brought you to Sumatra and India. Among many other wonders you meet a unicorn, but it's nothing like the gentle creature people back home suppose it is.

The omens are fine. Can I come down now?

YOU'VE COME FROM CATHAY by ship. The crew wouldn't set off if the omens weren't good. To find out, they strap a man to a kite and see whether he gets airborne. They won't sail if he doesn't.

THERE'S A REALLY YUMMY sweet in Sumatra, made from stuff called sago. It comes from the soft spongy part of a palm tree.

Snort!

UGH! Creepy crawlies! In India, people hoist their beds to the ceiling by ropes, to escape tarantulas.

The cool way to keep sharks away while pearl-fishing is to hire a Brahmin to chant spells. Give him one pearl for every 20 you find.

This really isn't how I imagined them at all!

MARCO ADMIRES the Indian yogis (below), who go naked and live on rice. Yogis will not kill any living thing. They won't even eat leaves unless they are withered, because they say all fresh things have souls.

OYSTERS with magnificent pearls are found in the gulf between India and Ceylon.* Divers hold their breath to bursting point to bring them up.

*now Sri Lanka

Escorting the princess

fter 17 years in the Khan's service you are all anxious to get home. But that doesn't suit the Khan; he's refusing to let such useful servants go. You're beginning to think you'll be prisoners here for ever when something happens to make him change his mind. The Khan of Persia asks for one of the royal princesses to be sent to him as a bride. She must be safely escorted to Persia. The aged Khan reluctantly decides that experienced travellers like the Polos are needed for the task.

Trust them, my dear.

THE KHAN provides a fleet of 14 ships to carry the princess and her attendants. There are 600 people aboard when you set sail, but only 16 will survive the terrible three-year voyage.

Handy hint

If you see smoke on the horizon, watch out! It means a pirate ship has spotted you and is signalling others to join the attack.

THE FLEET is marooned for five months in Sumatra, waiting for favourable winds. Some of the islanders are said to be cannibals. You build a stockade on the beach to keep them out, just in case it's true.

DISEASE AND DISASTERS dog the voyage. Crossing the Indian Ocean, you find yourselves at the mercy of pirates from the Gujarat Coast, who comb the seas in well-organised fleets.

I don't believe it either.

A NASTY PIRATE TRICK! Merchants who may have swallowed gems to hide them are made to drink a mixture of tamarind and sea water till they vomit them up.

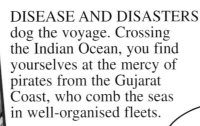

Gulp!

HERE'S A TALE you find hard to believe, yet sailors swear it's true. On islands off the coast of Africa there are gigantic birds that prey on elephants. They kill them by dropping them from a height.

Welcome home!

The trip home has not been a total disaster. The princess has been safely delivered, and after 24 years you are in back in Venice at last. People stare at your weather-beaten faces and travel-stained Mongol clothes. When the Polos knock on the door of their house they are told to clear off! It takes time to convince the family that they really are the long-lost Niccolò, Maffeo and Marco, returned as rich men from serving the ruler of half the world. Who's going to believe such stories?

Oh no you're not!

Oh yes we are!

Knock Knock

SOME OF MARCO'S SOUVENIRS: silky yak's hair, the dried head and feet of a musk deer, and seeds of Sumatran indigo (Marco planted them but they didn't grow).

Handy hint

When you've seen wonders that are almost beyond belief, don't get too upset if people won't believe you.

SOME SAY that Marco stunned his doubting family by slitting pouches in his travelling clothes and spilling out cascades of precious stones.

MARCO HAS WRITTEN an account of his travels (dictated while a prisoner of war in Genoa). People say that it's a lot of boasting. Well, some of it may be, but a lot of it is true – you were there!

Right: Chapter 24...

Glossary

Bile A green, bitter liquid produced by a small gland just below the liver.

Brackish Slightly salty and unpleasant to drink.

Brahmin A member of the priestly class in Hinduism.

Buddha In the Buddhist religion, a person who has achieved a state of perfect enlightenment.

Caravan A group of merchants travelling together for safety.

Cathay In Marco Polo's time, a name for what is now northern China.

Concubine A secondary wife, of inferior status to a main wife.

Depot A storehouse for goods.

Envoy A person sent to deliver an official message, or to discuss a matter on behalf of the sender.

Falconry Using trained hawks to hunt birds and small mammals.

Galley A ship powered by both oars and sails.

Goitre A swelling of the thyroid gland in the neck, often caused by a lack of iodine in the body.

Holy oil Oil burnt in the lamp of the Church of the Holy Sepulchre in Jerusalem.

Indigo A plant that produces a highly valued blue dye.

Jade A pale green gemstone.

Khan The title given to the ruler of some Asian countries.

Kublai Khan (1215–1294) Mongol emperor and grandson of Genghis Khan. He extended Mongol rule into southern China and adopted the highly civilised Chinese way of life.

Mange A skin disease of hairy animals, caused by parasitic mites.

Marauders A group of travelling thieves, bandits.

Mongols Nomadic herdsmen of central Asia who united in the early 13th century under a conquering warlord, Genghis Khan. They created one of the largest empires in history, stretching from the Pacific Ocean to the Black Sea.

Mount Ararat A mountain in present-day Turkey, traditionally supposed to be the place where Noah's ark came to rest after the flood.

Musk deer A small Asian deer that has no antlers.

Omen An object or event that is supposed to be a sign of future good or evil.

Pamir Mountains A region of central Asia with some of the highest mountain ranges on earth. After Marco Polo's time, they were not explored by Westerners till 1871.

Pavilion A large, extravagant tent.

Pope The head of the Roman Catholic church.

Seal A design that is stamped on documents to prove that the documents have been issued by the owner of the seal.

Steppes Vast, treeless plains of northern Asia.

Tamarind Acid-tasting pulp from the pods of the tamarind tree.

Tarantula A name applied to various kinds of large spiders.

Turkestan The historical name of a vast central Asian region which includes modern Turkmenistan, Tajikistan, Uzbekistan and a part of western China.

Turquoise A blue-green gemstone.

Yak An Asian wild ox with long hair hanging nearly to the ground.

Yogi A person who lives by the principles of yoga, a way of achieving spiritual enlightenment through meditation.

Index